THE CRAFT COMPANION

ABOUT THE AUTHOR

Dorothy Morrison is a Wiccan High Priestess of the Georgian Tradition. She founded the Coven of the Crystal Garden in 1986. An avid practitioner of the Ancient Arts for more than twenty years, she spent many years teaching the Craft to students throughout the United States and Australia and is a member of the Pagan Poet's Society.

An archer and bow hunter, Dorothy regularly competes in outdoor tournaments and holds titles in several states. Her other interests include tarot work, magical herbalism, stonework, and computer networking.

TO WRITE TO THE AUTHOR

If you wish to contact the author or would like more information about this book, please write to the author in care of Llewellyn Worldwide and we will forward your request. Both the author and publisher appreciate hearing from you and learning of your enjoyment of this book and how it has helped you. Llewellyn Worldwide cannot guarantee that every letter written to the author can be answered, but all will be forwarded. Please write to:

Dorothy Morrison
℅ Llewellyn Worldwide
P.O. Box 64383, Dept. 0-7387-0093-2
St. Paul, MN 55164-0383, U.S.A.

Please enclose a self-addressed stamped envelope for reply,
or $1.00 to cover costs. If outside U.S.A., enclose
international postal reply coupon.

Many of Llewellyn's authors have websites with additional information and resources. For more information, please visit our website at http://www.llewellyn.com.

THE CRAFT
COMPANION

A WITCH'S JOURNAL

DOROTHY
MORRISON

2001
Llewellyn Publications
St. Paul, Minnesota 55164-0383, U.S.A.

FIRST EDITION
Second Printing, 2001

Book design and editing by Karin Simoneau
Cover design by Lisa Novak
Interior illustrations © 2001 by Kate Thomssen

Library of Congress Cataloging-in-Publication Data
Morrison, Dorothy, 1955-
  The craft companion: a witch's journal / Dorothy Morrison.
    p.   cm.
  ISBN 0-7387-0093-2
  1. Witchcraft. 2. Spiritual journals—Authorship—Miscellanea. I. Title.

BF1566 .M745   2001   2001020384

Llewellyn Publications
A Division of Llewellyn Worldwide, Ltd.
P.O. Box 64383, Dept. 0-7387-0093-2
St. Paul, MN 55164-0383, U.S.A.
www.llewellyn.com

 Printed on recycled paper in the United States of America

Other Books by Dorothy Morrison

Magical Needlework
Llewellyn Publications, 1998

Everyday Magic
Llewellyn Publications, 1998

In Praise of the Crone: A Celebration of Feminine Maturity
Llewellyn Publications, 1999

The Whimsical Tarot
Deck and book; U.S. Games Systems Inc., 2000

Yule: A Celebration of Light & Warmth
Llewellyn Publications, 2000

Bud, Blossom, & Leaf: The Magical Herb Gardener's Handbook
Llewellyn Publications, 2001

The Craft: A Witch's Book of Shadows
Llewellyn Publications, 2001

HOW TO USE THIS BOOK

As I wrote *The Craft,* I realized that folks would need a place to record exercise notes, track study progress, and plan their spells and rituals. I thought of adding blank pages, but scrapped the idea as soon as it entered my head. The reason was simple: Since most folks absolutely refuse to write in their text books, adding pages that no one would really use was just a waste of paper.

That being the case, something else was necessary. Something entirely different. Something with lots of blank pages that simply begged to be written upon. The answer was a journaling tool of sorts—and to that end, *The Craft Companion* was born.

While this book can definitely be used to record exercise notes and track magical progress, its usefulness doesn't stop there. Because it contains more than a hundred spells and magical ideas, *The Craft Companion* goes one step further. It also provides the perfect tool for starting your very first Book of Shadows—and that's something very special, indeed.

To use this book in such a fashion, begin by choosing one of the spells inside. Just write down the current day of the week (Monday, Tuesday, Wednesday, and so on) and the phase of the moon (dark, waxing, full, or waning). If you have an ephemeris at your disposal, you may wish to check the sign of the moon and jot it down as well. Since particular signs are more fruitful than others, this information could prove useful later when checking your results.

Next, write down the time and perform the spell.

Afterward, make notes of everything you did and everything that happened. Notice the candle flame, for example. Did it flicker, dance, or just burn strong and true? Jot down other things, too. Things like fleeting thoughts, mental pictures, or physical exhaustion. Did anything unusual happen? This could be as simple as a falling leaf or as complex as an unexpected vision or message. All these things are important. And all of them need to be recorded.

Finally, record the results. Did the spell work or not? (Be aware that magic usually works in twenty-one days or not at all.) If it did, mark the page with a star or some other special symbol. That way, you'll know to perform the spell in exactly the same way should you ever choose to use it again.

If it didn't, though, don't fret. Just go back to the information you wrote down. First, check to see if there was a problem with the day of the week or the moon phase. A love spell, for instance, has a better chance of success if performed under a waxing or full moon. Its chances of manifestation also increase if it's performed on Friday, the day of Venus, the Goddess of Love. That being the case, make some appropriate notes so you'll be able to increase your success ratio the next time you perform the spell.

Don't be afraid to use the book to record other magical data as well. Jot down an incense recipe here, an herbal remedy there, the details of a dream, or maybe even a poem that meandered through your brain during daily meditation. That is, after all, what compiling a Book of Shadows is all about: the chronicling of your steps on the personal path—a path like no other—a path that you, alone, design as you discover the wonders and mysteries of the magical life.

REDE OF THE WICCA

Bide the Wiccan Law you must, in perfect love and perfect trust.

Live and let live; fairly take and fairly give.

Cast the Circle thrice about, to keep all evil spirits out.

To bind the spell every time, let the spell be spake in rhyme.

Soft of eye and light of touch, speak little and listen much.

Deosil go by the waxing Moon, sing and dance the Witches' Rune.

Widdershins go when the Moon doth wane, and werewolf howls by the dread wolfsbane.

When the Lady's Moon is new, kiss thy hand to Her times two.

When the Moon rides at Her peak, then your heart's desire speak.

Heed the Northwind's mighty gale, lock the door and drop the sail.

When the wind comes from the South, love will kiss thee on the mouth.

When the Westwind blows o'er thee, departed spirits restless be.

Nine woods in the cauldron go, burn them fast and burn them slow.

Elder be the Lady's tree—burn it not, or cursed be!

When the Wheel begins a turn, let the Beltane fires burn.

When the Wheel hath turned to Yule, light the log and let Pan rule.

Heed ye flower, bush, and tree, and by the Lady, Blessed Be!

Where the rippling waters flow, cast a stone and truth you'll know.

Whenever ye have a need, harken not to others' greed.

With the fool, no seasons spend, nor be counted as his friend.

Merry Meet and Merry Part, bright the cheeks and warm the heart.

Mind the Threefold Law ye should, three times bad an' three times good.

When misfortune is enow, wear the Blue Star on your brow.

True in love ever be, unless thy love is false to thee.

Eight words the Wiccan Rede fulfill: "An' it harm none, do what ye will!"

STONE SPELL FOR PROPHETIC DREAMS

For dreams filled with prophesy or visions of the future, all you need is a small piece of citrine. Hold the stone firmly between your palms and enchant it by saying:

Stone of wonder, stone of might
Stone that shines deep in the night
Shine into the future deep
And bring its visions while I sleep

Continue to hold the stone until you feel a pulsing sensation, then place it beneath your pillow (inside the case). Prophetic dreams will come for as long as it stays there.

TO DETERMINE IF THE OBJECT OF YOUR AFFECTIONS IS TRUE TO YOU

Pick a sprig of basil (or purchase the fresh herb at your local supermarket) on the new moon. Enchant it by saying:

Basil, basil, hear my plea
Do now what I ask of thee
Stay fresh and green if love is true
But shrivel if it's not on cue

Place the sprig into the hand of the one you love. If it shrivels up right away, someone else holds the key to his or her heart. If it doesn't, your love is true to you.

FOR GENERAL FINANCIAL GAIN

For this spell, you'll need a penny, nickel, dime, and quarter, and a green candle. Wait until a Thursday morning, then arrange the coins around the candle in a circle. Light the candle and say:

> *Bring cash—now send it on its way*
> *Bring it now. Right here. Today.*

Visualize yourself being surrounded by money. Let the candle burn all the way down. Carry the coins with you.

SPELL TO KINDLE ROMANCE

To bring about romance that makes you weak in the knees, gather six red rose buds and a pink candle. Arrange the rose buds in the shape of a heart in front of the candle, then light the wick as you chant:

> *Venus, Goddess of Romance*
> *Help me in this loving dance*
> *Give me what I most desire*
> *By the light of candle fire*

After the candle burns out, place the rose buds in your pillowcase.

MORNING THANKSGIVING PRAYER

To ensure a joyous and productive day, start each morning by lighting a white candle and saying the following prayer. You'll be amazed at the blessings you'll receive!

I give You thanks for all You do
For obstacles, and smooth roads, too
For challenges that make me grow
And all the pleasant things that show
That You are looking after me
I thank You, Ancients! Blessed be!

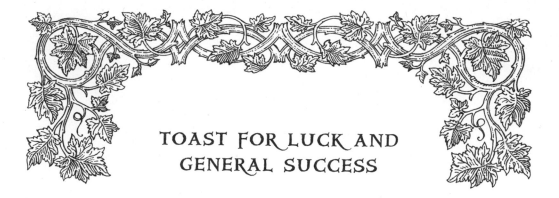

TOAST FOR LUCK AND GENERAL SUCCESS

To obtain the Sun's blessings of good luck and general success, rise just before dawn. Fill a glass with orange juice and take it outside, facing East. Just as the Sun crests the horizon, hold the glass high and toast the Sun by saying:

O mighty Sun of warmth and light
O Sun of power and of might
Look down on me this gorgeous day
And send good fortune now my way

A BLESSING FOR KITCHEN HERBS

To bless kitchen herbs, rise at dawn and gather the
herbs together on the kitchen counter. Hold your
hands above them (palms down) and say:

> *God and Goddess of the good Earth*
> *Bless these herbs with love and mirth*
> *And as their powers are released*
> *Let them flavor well each feast*

A CHANT FOR CREATIVITY

To unblock personal inspiration and creativity, try the chant below. The results are more than just successful—they're immediate!

Minerva and Athena!
Grant me now Your panacea
Bring ideas into the flow
And let creative urges grow

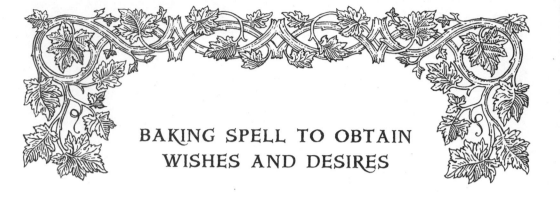

BAKING SPELL TO OBTAIN WISHES AND DESIRES

To obtain your most heartfelt desires, begin by baking something—cookies, cake, pie, bread—in honor of Vesta, the Goddess of Hearth and Fire. As the item cools, enchant it by saying:

Vesta of the hearth and fire
Bring to me what I desire
Grant your blessings on this fodder
That I consume now in Your honor

Eat some of the baked goods, and know that Vesta will bring your wishes to fruition.

THE WISHING WELL

To make the wishing well, you'll need a small fish bowl, some aquarium gravel or small stones, and an assortment of pennies. Fill the bowl half-full of gravel, and add water to the top. When the water clears, make a wish and toss in a penny while saying the following chant to Domna, Keeper of the Sacred Stones.

Domna of the Sacred Stones
I send this wish to You, alone
Bring results right back to me
As I will, so mote it be

EARTH APPRECIATION SPELL

Today, give something back to Mother Earth for all that She gives you. This gift doesn't have to be extravagant. Some mulch, a bit of cornmeal, some fertilizer sticks, or a few pennies will do. As you plant your gift in the ground, kiss the Earth and softly say:

Mother Earth, I give to You
This small gift for all You do
Take it, please, and smile on me
As I walk Your path now. Blessed be!

BLESSING FOR PRIVACY

To enchant your favorite resting place or personal space for privacy, just stand in the doorway and ask the Lady for help by saying:

O Lovely Lady, lend an ear
And grant me privacy in here
So those who look for me can't see
Grant invisibility

SPELL FOR STRONG FAMILY BONDS OR LASTING FRIENDSHIPS

Begin this spell by presenting each family member or friend with an acorn. Once everyone has their acorn, have them join hands in a circle and ask the blessing of the oak by saying together:

We honor you, O Mighty Oak
Grant your strength unto these folks
Let it surge throughout these seeds
And make us strong in thought and deed

Then ask each person to carry their acorn charms with them at all times. As they do, the bonds between them will grow and solidify.

SPELL TO CALL THE FAIRIES AND FEY

To call fairies, fey, and other wee folk to you, all you need is a shiny dime and a couple of table-spoons of dried thyme. Just hold the dime and herbs in your hand, then invoke them by saying:

I call on You who fly and flit
To talk with me for just a bit
And in return, I'll give this thyme
And this shimmering, silvery dime

After they come and you've had time to chat a bit, toss the money and herbs on the wind. (Be sure to keep the gifts in your hand until you're ready for them to leave. The fey are sly folk and won't stay long unless you have something that they want!)

SPELL TO KEEP FROM RUNNING OUT OF GAS

If you get stuck in traffic on the way to the service station and it looks like you might run out of gas, try the following chant while visualizing the fuel expanding inside your tank. It will keep you moving until you find the fuel pump.

Gods of petrol, fuel, and gas
Expand my fuel and do it fast!

CHANT FOR BETTER COMMUNICATION SKILLS

To dispel troubles with oral or written communication, call on Sarasvati, the Goddess of Eloquence, by chanting:

O Sarasvati, come right now
I need Your help, so please allow
The honor of Your presence here
Let all my words ring loud and clear

SPELL FOR PERSONAL POWER

To increase your personal power, take a yard of string, ribbon, or yarn, and tie a knot in its center while saying:

I am power; I'm divine
I am God/dess by design
I am all there is to be
Power's mine. So mote it be!

Repeat this spell for eight more days, tying knots of equal distance until there are nine. Then put the cord in a safe place and wear it on the Sabbats.

SPELL TO BRING RAIN

To bring rain, wait until a sunny morning, then pick a handful of ferns. Burn the ferns to ash while continuously chanting the following verse.

Bring us rain and bring it fast
Soothe this parching drought at last
But bring us only what we need
So all are safe within this deed

When the ashes are cool, scatter them on the ground and visualize the rain washing them away.

SPELL FOR A SPECIAL NEED

On a night when the moon is waxing, gather nine
stones (all different colors) and a white candle.
Light the candle, then enchant each stone with the
following verse.

Bring to me my heart's desire
By Elements of Air and Fire
By Water Element, as well
Of which the concentrated gel
Makes Your existence and the Earth
I ask you this in love and mirth

Place the stones on the altar in front of the candle,
and allow the wick to burn down completely.
Then bury the stones in the ground.

SPELL FOR HEALING

For this spell, all you need is a glass of water. Take it to wherever you are most comfortable—the couch, the kitchen table, or the bed, for example—and relax. Then blow across the water's surface and say:

I heal myself of (problem)
With this water, I am free
By the power of Ancients
And my will, so mote it be

When you are finished, drink the water and know that healing is on its way.

SIMPLE SPELL BINDING

To keep all safe from harm during spellwork, use the following binding chant with every magical effort you perform.

> *By karmic power of number three*
> *This spell tied and knotted be*
> *So that its contents stay together*
> *And can't harm human, beast, or weather*

DANDELION SPELL FOR PSYCHIC POWER

Go outside on a sunny day and pick some dande-
lions, then fashion them into a small wreath. As
you place the wreath on your head, invoke the
spirit of the dandelion by saying something like:

O little crown of flowers, gold
Help me see what I'm not told
Let me feel and hear it, too
Do now what I ask of you!

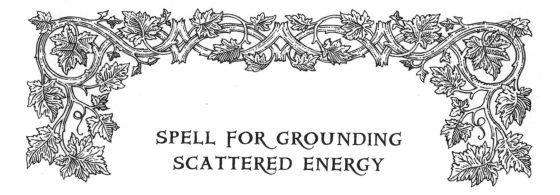

SPELL FOR GROUNDING SCATTERED ENERGY

To stabilize your energy, fill a small jar with soil. (Baby food or spice jars work well for this.) Then call on Mother Earth by chanting:

Mother Earth, solid One
Kissed by rain, and wind, and Sun
Bring stable balance unto me
As I will, so mote it be

Keep the jar close by—in your purse or at the workplace, for example—and nervous energy won't be a problem.

CHANT FOR INSPIRATION

When fresh ideas and inspiration can't be found,
try this quick chant to the Muses. They'll come to
your aid immediately.

Muses come from far and near
I command You! Listen! Hear!
From North and East and South and West
Come and do what You do best
Bring ideas and let them flow
As I will, it shall be so

PERSONAL PATH SPELL

To bring about positive changes in your personal path, take a handful of pennies and go outside. Then walk down the street and drop a penny in honor of Elena, Goddess of Paths and Roads. As you drop the coin, say:

Elena, Goddess of the Road
Who bears all weight and heavy load
I honor you in this small way
And thank you for this path today

Continue to drop pennies one at a time, repeating the chant as you go.

CHAOS REMOVAL CHANT

When the business of everyday living gets to be more than you can handle and chaos seems to peek out from every corner, try this quick chant to calm things down. Just lie down on your bed, shake your fist toward the ceiling, and shout as loudly as you can:

Make mischief somewhere else today
You can no longer stay and play
I have no room in here for you
Go else I kick you black and blue

NIGHTMARE REMOVAL
SPELL

To keep nightmares at bay, hold a piece of citrine
in your hand while visualizing peaceful sleep and
gentle dreams. Then hold the stone to your Third
Eye (the spot between your eyebrows) and say:

As I go to sleep at night
Exterminate dreams that bring me fright
Keep them far away from me
As I will, so mote it be

Place the stone beneath your bed and nightmares
will be a thing of the past.

TO SEE PAST LIVES

To see past lives, stand or sit in front of a mirror
on the first night of the dark moon and say:

> *Bring visions of the lessons learned*
> *In my past lives; I have earned*
> *The right to see them, so allow*
> *Vivid details—bring them now*

Then look closely in the mirror and watch as your
past lives play out within it.

PERSONAL PROPERTY
PROTECTION SPELL

To protect your home from theft, it's a good idea to bless all the locks and keys in your home. Just place your hands on each item and call on Syn and Carna, the Goddesses of Doors and Locks, by saying:

Carna and Syn of locks and doors
Bless these devices evermore
Make them work—keep all secure
From harm and hurt and evildoers

SPELL TO SEE
BEAUTY IN LIFE

When you're feeling down and out, just hold a
piece of unakite between your hands and enchant
it by saying:

Stone of beauty, pink and green
Show me what I haven't seen
All that life shall offer me
As I will, so mote it be

Carry the stone with you, and see how quickly the
positive aspects of your life become apparent.

DROUGHT PREVENTION SPELL

To prevent a drought, just sprinkle a glass of water on the ground. Watch it disappear into the Earth and say:

Water, soak the dry, parched ground
So a good supply is always found
By my will, there be no drought
Earth, stay moist both in and out

SALT PROTECTION SPELL

Since negative energies and entities cannot cross salt, it's the best protection device available. That being the case, sprinkle salt along both the inner and outer perimeters of your home while saying:

Negative energy, go away
For in salt's presence you can't stay
Bane be gone away as well
I banish you by salty spell

PROTECTION BATH

When troubles come your way, fill the bathtub
with warm water and toss in a handful of salt. As
you step in, call on Aegir, the God of the Rolling
Sea, and ask for His protection by saying:

Aegir of the rolling sea
Keep Your watchful eyes on me
Protect me with Your precious salt
And keep me far from harm and fault

CHANT FOR
INNER STRENGTH

To gain inner strength and courage, say the following chant to Hercules, the God of Strength. Repeat the chant on each odd hour from the time you rise until the time you go to bed.

Hercules, come be with me
With Your power, set me free

CHANT FOR HELP DURING A DIFFICULT TASK

Should you lack the self-confidence to handle something that comes your way, use the following chant to invoke Heimdall, the God Who lights the bridge between life and death. He will guide your way and show you which steps to take.

Heimdall, show me what to do
Heimdall, stick to me like glue
Guide and show me what I need
To successfully complete this deed

SPELL FOR
PERSONAL OPPORTUNITY

During a new to full moon, anoint all your doors
with a dab of peach oil. Then call on Janus, the
God of Opportunity, by saying:

Janus, open up Your doors
Bring me the break I'm looking for
Bring me opportunity
As I will, so mote it be

SPELL FOR
MONETARY INCREASE

To fertilize money and make it grow, place your loose change in a dish and take it outdoors. (Make sure you have at least one penny, nickel, dime, and quarter in the pile.) Hold the dish up to the sky and invoke the Maiden by saying:

> *Money multiply and grow*
> *Fertile Maiden, make it so*
> *Let money multiply with ease*
> *With the help of Blessed Be's*

Then, repeating the chant with each coin, plant a penny, nickel, dime, and quarter in the ground, while visualizing the money growing. Take the dish back inside and put it in a place where you'll see it often. Feed it a few coins every day.

CHANT TO REGAIN A SENSE OF HUMOR

When you find yourself taking life too seriously, take a minute to laugh. Then say this chant to Loki, the God of Tricks and Fun. Your sense of humor will return in nothing flat.

Loki, God of Tricks and Fun
Bring me help now on the run
Bring joyous mischief I can feel
Bring me laughter—make it real

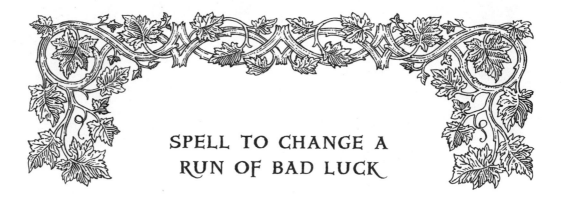

SPELL TO CHANGE A
RUN OF BAD LUCK

Begin by standing with your back firmly against a wall. Take a moment to gather all your strength, courage, and power. Then take one step out from the wall and invoke Fortuna, the Goddess of Luck, by yelling the following at the top of your lungs:

Lady Luck, Fortuna, dear,
Make my bad luck disappear
I've had enough—chase it away
Bring to me good luck today

BREAD AND GRAIN
HEALTH SPELL

Gather all your bread and grain products—flour, cornmeal, oatmeal, crackers, popcorn, and so on—and place them on the kitchen counter. Hold your hands over them, palms down, then bless them in the name of Ceres, the Goddess of Grain, by saying:

> *I bless these, Ceres, in Your name*
> *These loaves and meals all made of grain*
> *And as they're consumed,*
> *bring lasting good health*
> *I thank you, Ceres, for Your wealth*

Afterward, scatter a few bread or cracker crumbs outside for the birds.

MULTIPURPOSE FREEDOM CHANT

This chant to Libertas, the God of Freedom, has many purposes. It can be used to chase away old ideas and bring fresh perspective. It can also be used for cutting ties that bind you, for removing obstacles from your path, or for relieving any sort of situation that keeps you from moving forward. The key to its success, however, is that you must say this chant with feeling and then take appropriate steps toward meeting your goals.

Libertas, please cut away
(Name of problem) that has come to stay
Grant now Your gift of liberty
So from this moment, I am free

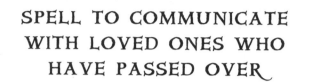

SPELL TO COMMUNICATE WITH LOVED ONES WHO HAVE PASSED OVER

For this spell, you'll need an opal or a small quartz crystal and a sparkling clean mirror. Hold the stone in your hand and stand before the mirror, saying:

> *Come to me all spirits of*
> *Family, friends, and ones I love*
> *Tell me what I need to know*
> *Tell me all before you go*

Then watch the mirror closely, as the spirits will materialize in its reflection.

ONGOING SPELL TO
HEAL THE EARTH

To heal the Earth, begin a compost heap to recycle grass clippings, leaves, fruit peel, egg shells, and so on. Add to the collection daily while chanting something like:

> *We chase away the good Earth's blues*
> *By recycling what we use*
> *It brings good health to Mother Earth*
> *And makes her smile in joy and mirth*

As the compost heap grows and is used, the Earth around you will begin to heal.

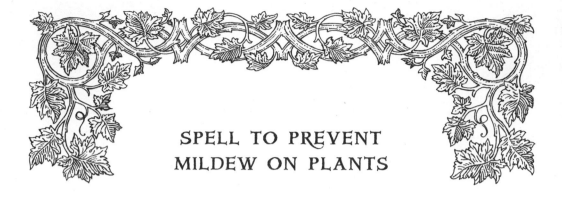

SPELL TO PREVENT MILDEW ON PLANTS

To perform this spell, add one teaspoon of baking soda to a quart of water on the first day of the new moon. Stir the mixture until all the soda is dissolved while chanting:

By love and light, by night and day
Mildew go! You cannot stay

Pour the mixture into a spray bottle, then mist all plants thoroughly as you repeat the chant. Mildew will no longer present a problem.

SPELL TO STOP CONFUSION

To clear confusion and see things as they really are, gather nine tacks or pushpins, then go outdoors and find a place beneath a tree. Plant the tacks' points up around the tree base, while saying with each placement:

Make my mind as sharp as tacks
Let me see now just the facts
Ground me with the Earth as well
Bring mental clarity with this spell

Cover the tacks well with soil, and confusion will become a thing of the past.

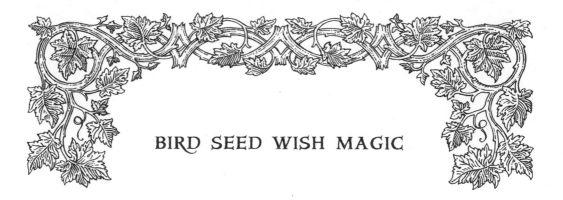

BIRD SEED WISH MAGIC

To bring a wish into reality, write your desire on a piece of paper. Fold the paper an odd number of times—one, three, or five, for example—and place it in a small dish. Cover the paper with bird seed while visualizing the wish coming true, then set the dish outside for the birds. Your wish should manifest within thirty days.

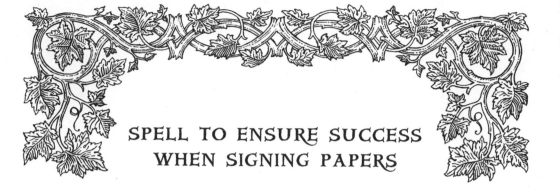

SPELL TO ENSURE SUCCESS WHEN SIGNING PAPERS

To bring success with contracts, business agreements, or any important papers that require your signature, turn the stack of papers face down. Then lick your finger and use it to draw a pentacle on each one. When all the papers are marked, bind the spell by saying something like:

By the Karmic Law of Three
I bind this spell to guarantee
That no harm shall come to me
But that success flows wild and free

TO DRAW A STINGER
FROM INSECT BITES

To quickly draw the stinger from bee, wasp, or other insect bites, moisten a teaspoon of baking soda with a few drops of vinegar to make a paste. Apply the paste to the affected area while saying:

Nasty stinger now be free
As I will, so mote it be

The stinger will be visible in a matter of minutes, and you'll be able to remove it with the tweezers.

STRESS REMOVAL SPELL

To get rid of troubles, worries, or whatever is bringing stress into your life, just grab a stack of blank paper and take it outside. Label each sheet with a worry and fold it into a paper airplane. Sail the airplanes into the air as fast as you can, and bury each one where it lands, saying:

Of these troubles I am free
As I will, so mote it be

SPELL TO BRING
NEW BUSINESS

When the moon is waxing, add five crushed bay leaves to a quart of boiling water. Remove the mixture from the stove and allow it to steep for twenty minutes. As it steeps, think of your business flourishing and chant something like:

Herbs and water, mix and flow
One into the other go
Become the magic that you know
And make my business thrive and grow

Use the mixture to paint the threshold, steps, and baseboards of your business space. While painting, chant:

Seven, five, three, one
Bring new business on the run

Repeat every three months.

CHANT FOR MOTIVATION

When you have tons of things to do, but can't seem to get going, the following chant will do the trick.

Get me moving—do it now
Increased vitality allow
Bring vim and vigor—make it stay
And chase all laziness away

SPELL TO REMOVE WARTS

To get rid of warts, just gather one penny for each wart, and a roll of adhesive tape. Holding your hands over the pennies, enchant them by saying:

Copper, take these warts from me
As I will, so mote it be

Then tape one coin over each wart. They'll be gone in about a week.

SPELL TO HELP THE
SEASONS CHANGE

To help the seasons change with ease, just find a
fallen stick. Point it toward the ground and move
it in a circular clockwise motion while saying:

Seasons change without the pain
Of birth; new strength I bid you, gain
From tree to ground—from sky to Earth
I bid you, change with love and mirth

Keep the stick in a safe place so you can use it
again to aid the next seasonal change.

WEIGHT LOSS SPELL

Enchant a piece of blue topaz during the waning
moon by saying:

Help me in my diet quest
Bring to me new strength and zest
Take these extra pounds from me
As I will, so mote it be

Your weight will drop gradually as you wear the
stone or carry it with you.

SHOWER SPELL FOR EMOTIONAL BALANCE

To restore emotional balance, begin by taking a shower in your normal fashion. After rinsing all soap from your body, close your eyes and stand under the running water for a few minutes. Visualize the water as yellow paint and allow it to cover your body with its color. Watch as the water turns to red, and allow it to cover the yellow. Then repeat the visualization with blue, green, and white. Finally, visualize the water taking its clear form again and rinsing you clean. Emotional balance will return.

SPELL TO STOP A TROUBLEMAKER

To stop someone from causing trouble for you, write their name upon a fallen leaf and place it in a zippered bag. Add a spoon of sugar and fill the bag with water. Then shake the bag well while saying nine times:

I am out of (name of troublemaker) head
His (her) ill-will toward me is shed

Zip the bag and place it in the freezer. You'll be problem-free (at least of this person) as long as the contents stay frozen.

FROM FOE TO FRIEND SPELL

To make a friend out of an enemy, write your name on one side of an ice cream stick and your enemy's name on the other. Then cut a five-pointed star out of pink paper and place both items into a jar with a screw-on lid. Fill the jar half with sugar, half with water, and tighten the lid. Shake the jar nine times each day for nine days while saying as sweetly as you can:

Sweet thoughts of me, sweet thoughts of me
Are in (name of enemy) mind constantly

Keep the jar in a safe place.

STONE SPELL TO RESTORE COMMON SENSE

To restore common sense in times of stress, hold a piece of black tourmaline to your forehead and enchant it by saying:

Bring me clarity of mind
To sort through problems, and all kinds
Of messes as they come my way
Keep my head on straight today
And bring me sensibility
As I will, so mote it be

Hold it in your hand when tough or complicated matters demand your attention. Solutions will come easily.

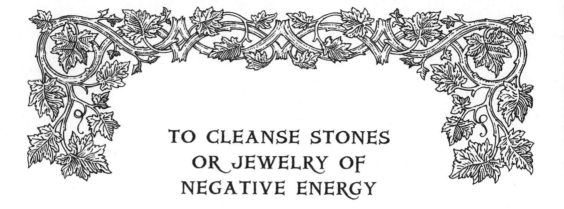

TO CLEANSE STONES
OR JEWELRY OF
NEGATIVE ENERGY

Wrap stones or jewelry carefully in plastic (zippered bags work well for this) and place them in your freezer. Leave them there for twenty-four hours, then remove. Negative energy will be a thing of the past.

PERSONAL SPACE BLESSING

To bless a personal space—a work room or an office, for example—light some incense and a white candle, and sprinkle the area with salted water. Then, beginning at the East side of the area and finishing at the North, move clockwise around the space in a circular motion while saying:

> *I cleanse you now within and out*
> *I sanctify you round about*
> *I cast out negative energy*
> *As I will so mote it be*

Repeat the movement and chant twice more, and let the candle burn all the way down.

AMULET, CHARM, AND TALISMAN BLESSING

Begin by gathering two candles of a color appropriate to your intention—pink for love, green for money, blue for tranquility, and so on—and place the object between them. Light the candles and say:

> *Grow in strength and grow in power*
> *Gain potency with every hour*
> *Gain what you need to do your task*
> *And accomplish everything I ask*
> *(state your magical purpose)*
> *is what I need of thee*
> *As I will so mote it be*

Leave the object in place until both candles completely burn down.

BATH SALTS FOR
LOVE AND ROMANCE

Begin on a Friday by pouring a cup of table salt
into a jar or a zippered, plastic bag. Add four
drops of jasmine oil, four drops of rose oil, and
one drop of cedar oil. Shake until well blended
while saying:

> *Love and romance come to me*
> *Make it all that it should be*
> *With your scent, attract and lure*
> *Love and romance, true and pure*

Add the mixture to your bath, then let your body
dry naturally.

TO GAIN RESPECT AT WORK

To gain the respect of employers and coworkers, hold a piece of turquoise in your hand and enchant it by saying:

> *Imbue this stone with trust in me*
> *Make coworkers quickly see*
> *That I am now part of their team*
> *And they should hold me in esteem*

Take the stone outdoors and bury it as close to the workplace building as possible.

ANGER DIFFUSION SPELL

Begin this spell by yelling and screaming as loud as you can. Then take a piece of paper and write down everything that brought you to this maddening state. Jot down every detail and be sure not to leave anything out. Then fold the paper three times and scream:

I am furious—I will not flee
But anger will—just wait and see

Burn the note to ashes and scatter them on the winds.

TO CALM THE NERVES

Add one cup of boiling water to a teaspoon of valerian root. Allow it to steep for ten minutes while singing a happy tune ("Who's Afraid of the Big Bad Wolf?" is my personal favorite). When the time is up, add a teaspoon of honey and stir the tea clockwise while saying:

Anxious thoughts now flee and run
Bring back good cheer, laughs, and fun

Drink the tea.

TO-DO SPELL

When your to-do list becomes overwhelming, just grab a candle—any color will do—and inscribe it with every item on the list. Then light the candle and say:

*Things to do just melt away
within this candle wax
Short work, today,
I'll make of you—I'll get you done at last*

Handle the items one by one, finishing each before starting the next. You'll be surprised at how quickly things go as the candle burns down.

PROMISE-KEEPING SPELL

If keeping promises or commitments is a problem for you, just fill a small jar with jelly beans or another small candy or treat. Then hold your hands over the jar and enchant the goodies by saying:

The promises I make, I keep
My integrity runs deep

Eat one or two of the treats every day, and promise-keeping will no longer present a problem.

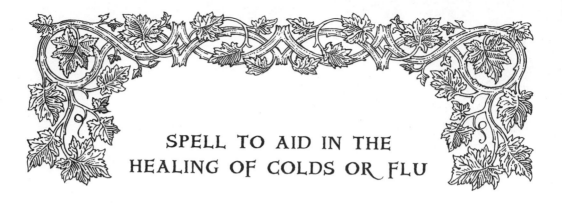

SPELL TO AID IN THE HEALING OF COLDS OR FLU

On a night during the waxing to full moon, mix a tablespoon of rue into a glass of water. The following night, take the glass outside and enchant the mixture beneath the moonlight by saying:

Herb of Grace, O cleansing one
Bring good health back on the run

Drink the water in its entirety.

PROTECTION FOR
LOVED ONES

Using a blender or a coffee grinder, blend together one teaspoon of mint, one teaspoon of clove, and one cup of baking soda while chanting:

> *Guard my loved ones—keep them sound*
> *Grant safety on air, sea, or ground*
> *Protect well their belongings, too*
> *Do now what I ask of you*

Then dust the mixture inside family member's shoes to ensure their safety.

HOUSEPLANT
GROWTH SPELL

Begin by gathering an assortment of clear quartz crystals, some cup hooks, and a supply of string, yarn, or ribbon. Attach a hook to the ceiling over each plant, then suspend the crystals from them by tying a string around each stone. As you suspend each crystal, say to the plant below:

Reach out—touch the stones, my dears
Grow and thrive with joy and cheer

Tend and nurture your plants in the usual fashion, and watch them grow.

MEAL BLESSING

It's just good manners to thank the Ancients for your food at mealtime. That being the case, use this simple blessing before you pick up your fork.

For this meal, I thank you now
As it sustains me, please allow
Your blessings on these gifts and me
As I will, so mote it be

SPELL TO INVITE THE FEY INTO YOUR HOME

Place four handkerchiefs on a flat surface, and sprinkle one teaspoon of thyme into the center of each. Knot each handkerchief to secure the thyme, then place one bundle in each corner of your home while saying:

I grant you entrance to my home
Come and frolic, play and roam

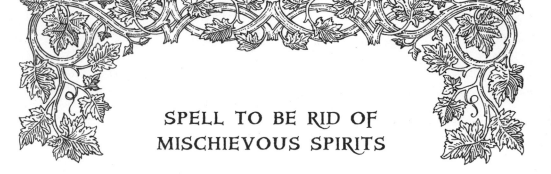

SPELL TO BE RID OF MISCHIEVOUS SPIRITS

Stand in the center of your home—or the area that
seems to be most affected—and hold your hands
up to the sky while saying three times:

> *Space I want and space there be*
> *Space between your bane and me*

Then light a vanilla candle to prevent their return.
Allow the candle to burn all the way down.

SPELL TO KEEP LOVE ALIVE

To keep love going in a current romance, light a red candle, then, using red ink, write the following words on white paper.

Venus! Mars! Come do Your thing
Into our hearts Your passion fling
I ask new breadth and depth, allow
Bring our love to life right now

Fold the paper in half, seal it with wax from the candle, and place it under your bed. Extinguish the candle.

MINOR ADDICTION/ BAD HABIT CHARM

Enchant a piece of staurolite (sometimes called fairy stone) during the waning moon by holding it to your forehead and saying:

Keep cravings far away from me
As I will, so mote it be

Carry the stone with you for quick results.

NEGATIVE ENERGY
REMOVAL SPELL

Begin by gathering as many small containers (margarine tubs work well for this) as there are rooms in your home. Place a slice of onion into each container and cover well with vinegar. Then place one dish in each room, saying:

Negative energy go away
By this spell you cannot stay
Begone from here now—fly and flee
As I will, so mote it be

ANXIETY REMOVAL SPELL

To rid yourself of undue anxiety or panic, light a vanilla candle and say three times:

Ease my pounding heart right now
Ease my nerves and don't allow
Anxiety to call again
Chase it back from whence it came

Visualize anxiety melting away with the candle wax. Let the candle burn all the way down.

APATHY RELIEF SPELL

Add one tablespoon of peppermint leaf to a cup of boiling water, then set it aside to steep for ten minutes. As it steeps, chant silently:

> *Add excitement, herb of spice*
> *Restore my interest in this life*
> *Indifference, now please chase away*
> *Remove this villain now, I say*

Drink the tea and feel indifference slip away.

ANTI-DOORMAT SPELL

If people seem to walk all over you or ignore your
accomplishments, obtain an arrowhead and rub it
well with lavender flowers while saying:

> *By Earth and plant, give credit due*
> *A new day's dawned, so bright and true*
> *I am worthy of respect*
> *By herb and stone, these thoughts reflect*

Carry the arrowhead or keep it near you, and the
problem will disappear.

CHANT TO BOOST CANDLE MAGIC

To add oomph to any spell involving candle magic, use the following chant when lighting the wick; then perform the spell as directed.

By dark of Crone and dark of night
I create this perfect light
Bring its power back to me
As I will, so mote it be

SPELL TO BOOST
PERSONAL PRODUCTIVITY

During the new to full moon, gather together a hematite, a quartz crystal, a piece of orange calcite, and a small basket or ash tray. Place the hematite in the container and enchant it by saying:

Ground and heal, magnetic one
Bring clarity 'til day is done

Add the quartz crystal and say:

Bring boundless energy my way
And let it last all through the day

Add the orange calcite and say:

Stone of joy and yellow light
Help me sort through workday plight

Place the container of stones on your desk and say:

Help me work 'til I am done
Bring inspiration on the run
So that when the day is through
I have nothing left to do

FULL MOON WISH SPELL

At night, when the moon is full, go outside with a glass of juice. Look up at the moon and tell it exactly what you desire. (Do this in full detail and don't leave anything out.) When you are done, lift your glass in toast to the moon and say:

> *Mother Goddess, look and see*
> *This goblet that I offer Thee*
> *It is Yours for all You do*
> *Gracious One of silver hue*

Pour the juice on the ground and know that your wish will be granted.

QUICK AMULET/
CHARM BLESSING

To bless an amulet or charm, hold it between your
hands and visualize the desired results in full
detail. Once the vision is imprinted in your mind's
eye, chant:

I give you joy and breath and life
I give you purpose, plan, and sight
Do now what I ask of thee
As I will, so mote it be

PROTECTION
AGAINST LIGHTNING

To protect your home from lightning strikes, form a cross with two rowan twigs by binding them together with red thread. Then ask Thor, the God of Lightning, for His blessing by saying:

Mighty Thor Who brings the fire
From sky to ground—from flame to pyre
I put this home now in Your care
Protect it well from lightning's fare

Hang the cross over your front door.

SPELL TO INCREASE PHYSICAL ENERGY

Hold a quartz crystal against your Third Eye (the spot between your eyebrows) and visualize your energy levels rising. Then take it one step further: see yourself with more energy than you can possibly use in one day. Still holding the stone to your Third Eye, chant:

> *Energy come and rise and stay*
> *Be enough for work and play*
> *With this stone now bonded be*
> *Increase my physical energy*

Wear the stone or carry it with you.

NEGATIVE ENERGY ABSORBER

Wash an egg in cold water, then dry it carefully and place it in a dish while chanting:

Absorb all negative energy
As I will, so mote it be

Put the dish under the bed close to the headboard. (If this isn't possible, place the dish in an area even with the location of your pillow.) Leave the dish for seven days, then bury the egg in the ground.

GENERAL PROTECTION
SPELL

When you need protection from that which you can't see, call on Artemis, the Goddess of All Wild Things, by using the following chant.

> *Lady of All Wild Things—*
> *Magic mistress of the night*
> *I chant Your name for all to hear—*
> *I ask You heed my plight*
> *Bring swift action, Artemis,*
> *and hold my hand this day*
> *Protect me from all harm*
> *that I encounter on my way*
> *Lend me courage as I tread this path*
> *I know as life*
> *And remove the obstacles that harm*
> *or cause me strife!*

To seal the spell, hold your arms up to the sky and chant the name "Artemis" three times.

TO LOCATE
MISSING OBJECTS

Try the following chant when you can't find your purse, keys, or other important items, and Expedite, the God of Missing Objects, will locate it for you.

> *Expedite, search and look*
> *Through every cranny, corner, nook*
> *Until You find this thing I need*
> *And I will pay you well, indeed*

The only hitch is that you must keep your promise of payment to Expedite. Just bury a dollar outside as an offering, and He will always come to your aid.

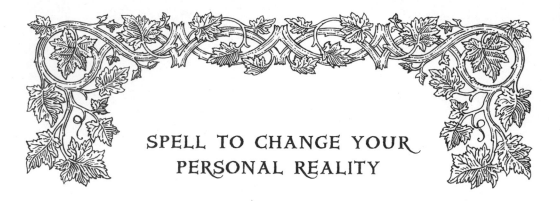

SPELL TO CHANGE YOUR PERSONAL REALITY

If life isn't going well and you feel the need to change your personal reality, grab some paper and a box of crayons or colored markers. Fill the paper with colored scribbles to signify the chaos in your current life. Then start the magic flowing by drawing a heavy black *X* across the whole sheet and saying:

> *I want no more of my old life*
> *No more dissension, stress, or strife*
> *Grant a new reality*
> *As I will, so mote it be*

To complete the spell, burn the paper and flush the ashes down the toilet.

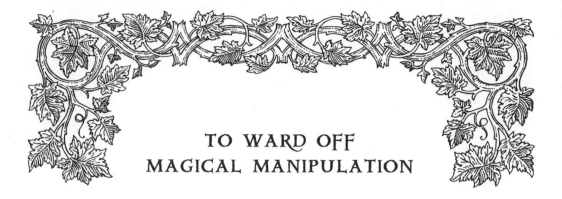

TO WARD OFF
MAGICAL MANIPULATION

If you have reason to believe that you're the victim of a spell or curse, just visualize yourself inside a silver ball and say:

Manipulations in my name
Bounce right back from whence they came
I'm protected in this sphere
From negative magic far and near

The effects of any magic directed at you will bounce right back to its sender.

KNOWLEDGE RETENTION CHARM

To retain knowledge and strengthen your memory,
enchant a piece of fluorite by saying:

> *Beauteous stone of color, rare*
> *Aid my memory with your fare*
> *Help me remember what I learn*
> *With every single page I turn*

Carry the stone with you or keep it in the area
where you work or study.

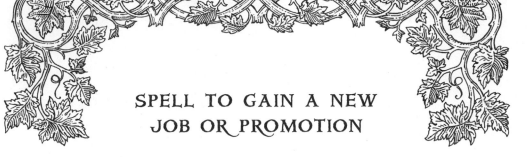

SPELL TO GAIN A NEW JOB OR PROMOTION

To secure a new job or gain a promotion, grab a piece of paper and write down all of your qualifications. Once you're done, fold the paper five times, chanting as you fold:

By fold of one, my wishes come
By fold of two, my dream comes true
By fold of three, the magic's free
By fold of four, it flies and soars
By fold of five, this spell's alive

Hide the paper in your purse or pocket, and take it with you to your interview.

ANTI-STUBBORNNESS SPELL

To open your mind, see new points of view, and squash your stubborn streak, begin by washing a piece of blue topaz in cold, clear water. As you dry the stone, chant:

Help me see new points of view
This, blue stone, I ask of you
Chase stubbornness away from me
As I will, so mote it be

Carry the stone with you.

TO REDUCE A FEVER

To bring down fever, hold your hands over the affected person and say three times within the hour:

Spirits dancing from the East
Bringing fire and ice and feast
In with ice and out with fire
Save the feast for health's desire

APPLE LOVE SPELL

To keep love growing strong and true, wait until the moon has waxed for three days. Wash a red apple in cold water, then polish it while saying:

Sweetest fire of fruit so red
Warm mind and heart, and turn the head

Kiss the apple six times, then give it to the one you love.

SAFE TRAVEL SPELL

Before embarking on a trip, invoke Mercury, the God of Travel, with the following chant. It guarantees safe passage and a pleasant journey to all involved.

Mercury, now hear my call
Grant safety to us one and all
Grant clear passage on the street
And a pleasant day to all I meet

HEARTH AND HOME PROTECTION SPELL

To keep your home free of chaos and havoc, grab five straws from your household broom. Light the straws, place them in a fireproof dish, then take the dish into each room, saying:

I give you heart and fire and light
With my breath I give you might
Protect all those who enter here
And bring them joy and love and cheer

When you're done, take the dish to the kitchen and leave it there until the straws burn to ash. Flush the ashes down the sink drain.

LUCK-CHANGING CHANT

When nothing seems to go your way, go outdoors on a night when the moon is waxing. Then call on Selene, the Goddess of the Night and the Moon, by saying:

Goddess of the Night and Moon
Change my luck and do it soon
Boost my strength and constitution
Bring to me a real solution

Blow a kiss to the moon, and know that everything will be alright.

ANTI-WEED SPELL

To keep your garden weed-free, yank a weed from the Earth, roots and all. Laugh and crush it in your hand, then toss it on the ground. Spit on it and sprinkle it heavily with salt while saying:

I stop you in your very tracks
You cannot hide and that's a fact
So take heed now, the rest of you
And move on, lest I crush you, too

TO PROTECT FROM DANGER

Should you find yourself in a potentially danger-
ous situation, kneel down, raise your arms to the
sky, and invoke Kali Ma by saying:

Kali Ma, I call on You
Do whatever You must do
To keep me safe from all that harms
Protect me in Your sacred arms

She will untangle you from the danger and protect
you from all harm.

SPELL TO
INCREASE FINANCES

To increase your cash flow and have enough for extra bills, light three candles—one yellow, one green, and one blue—and place seven pennies around them in a circle. Focus on the candle flames for a moment, then chant:

Increase my money—let it come
By moonlit night and daily Sun
Bring just enough that I may pay
The bills I owe from day to day

Let the candles burn completely down, then put the pennies in your purse or pocket. As long as you don't spend them, bills will never present a problem.

SELF-CONFIDENCE SPELL

Should self-confidence need a boost, write the following words on a piece of paper:

Confidence, come unto me
Nervousness, now quickly flee
Bring me strength and bring me ease
As I will, so mote it be

Place a piece of turquoise, hematite, and quartz crystal on top, then wrap the paper around the stones and secure the bundle with tape. Place the package in your purse or pocket to complete the spell.

ANTI-BOREDOM SPELL

If you feel you need some excitement in your life,
just plant a flower seed in the name of Nephthys,
Goddess of the Tomb. As you plant, say:

Clever Goddess of the Tomb
Grow excitement in Your womb
Bring surprises unto me
As I will so mote it be

(*Note:* Be absolutely sure that you want change
before doing this spell, for Nephthys has a strange
sense of humor and often brings more excitement
than one can imagine!)

PET PROTECTION SPELL

To protect dogs, cats, and other collar-wearing pets, just loop a hematite ring through the collar, and chant:

By light of moon and light of day
Be thou safe in work and play
Be thou happy and feel loved
Protected by the Gods above

NEW HOME PROTECTION

When claiming a new dwelling place, write the following words on a piece of paper and hang the paper over the front door to protect against thieves and burglars.

Who comes to me I keep
Who goes from me I free
Yet against all I stand
Who carry not my key

JUSTICE SPELL

When legal matters are a problem, or you feel that
you've been wronged in some way, invoke Hecate,
the Goddess of Justice, by chanting:

Keeper of what's just and right
Come and save me from this plight
Take swift action—hear my plea
Do now what I ask of Thee

Know that the problem will be resolved.

MAGICAL SOLSTICE
BOOSTER

The most magically powerful time of the year falls at noon on the solstice days (the first day of summer and the first day of winter). For an extra boost to all spells performed on these days, close the magical efforts with the following chant. Your magic will absolutely soar into the Universe.

By Air, by Earth, by Fire, by Water
By half, by cross, by season's quarter
Boost this magic—shell to core—
In double time and make it soar

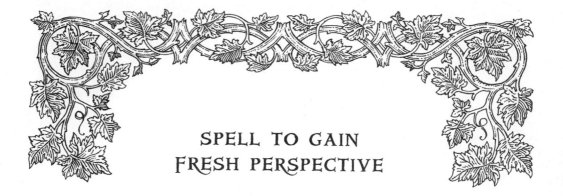

SPELL TO GAIN
FRESH PERSPECTIVE

When the moon is waxing, gather together a yellow candle, some vanilla oil, and a teaspoon of thyme. Anoint the candle with a bit of oil, then roll it in the thyme. Anoint your temples with a drop or two of oil, and light the candle while chanting something like:

Ancients come from near and far
Hear my call from where e'er you are
Propose, inspire, enchant, enthuse
Until I am at last infused
With new ideas and clear directive
Fill me with a fresh perspective

Let the candle burn down completely.

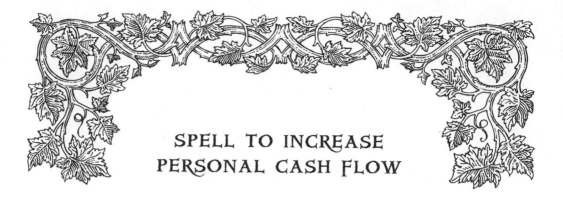

SPELL TO INCREASE PERSONAL CASH FLOW

During the waxing or full moon, hold a piece of aventurine in your dominant hand and concentrate on money flowing to you. Enchant the stone by saying something like:

Money come and money grow
Into my wallet gush and flow
And fill it to the very top
Then keep on coming—never stop

Place the stone in your pocket or purse, and carry it with you constantly.

AUTOMOBILE PROTECTION SPELL

Using your finger, mark a pentagram over each tire. Then get behind the wheel and visualize a blue pentagram hovering over the vehicle with the top point directly in the center of the hood. "Stretch" the pentagram until it completely wraps the vehicle and its points meet in the center of the chassis. As you visualize, chant something like:

Star of magic, star of power
Increase your potency with each hour
Protect this vehicle and me
As I will, so mote it be

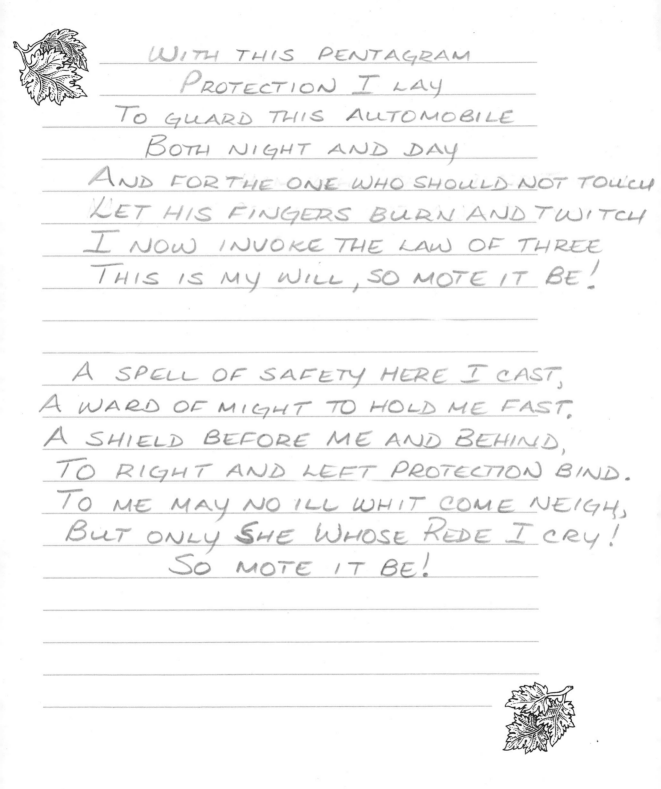

WITH THIS PENTAGRAM
PROTECTION I LAY
TO GUARD THIS AUTOMOBILE
BOTH NIGHT AND DAY
AND FOR THE ONE WHO SHOULD NOT TOUCH
LET HIS FINGERS BURN AND TWITCH
I NOW INVOKE THE LAW OF THREE
THIS IS MY WILL, SO MOTE IT BE!

A SPELL OF SAFETY HERE I CAST,
A WARD OF MIGHT TO HOLD ME FAST,
A SHIELD BEFORE ME AND BEHIND,
TO RIGHT AND LEFT PROTECTION BIND.
TO ME MAY NO ILL WHIT COME NEIGH,
BUT ONLY SHE WHOSE REDE I CRY!
SO MOTE IT BE!

DAILY PRAYER TO
THE GODDESS

Said on a daily basis, this prayer not only brings
boundless blessings from the Goddess, but seems
to hold life's little annoyances at bay.

Bless me, Goddess, on this day
Help me as I work and play
To reflect Your beauty now
Lend Your strength and please allow
This day to be all it should be
In love I ask this. Blessed be!

GLOSSARY OF DEITIES USED IN THIS BOOK

Aegir: God of the Rolling Sea

Ancients: Term used for the Collective Godhead

Artemis: Goddess of Wild Places, Animals, and Hunting

Athena: Goddess of Arts, Crafts, and War

Carna: Goddess of Locks

Ceres: Goddess of Grain

Crone: Goddess of Wisdom and Death; third and eldest phase of the Triple Goddess

Domna: Keeper of the Sacred Stones and Cairns

Elena: Goddess of Paths and Roadways

Expedite: God of Missing Objects

Fortuna: Goddess of Luck and Good Fortune

Hecate: Goddess of Justice

Heimdall: Light-bearing God Who guides those traveling the bridge between life and death

Hercules: God of Strength

Janus: God of Opportunity

Kali Ma: Goddess of Destruction

Libertas: God of Freedom

Loki: God of Tricks, Fun, and Mischief

Mars: God of War and Masculinity

Mercury: God of Communications, Business, and Travel

Minerva: Goddess of Arts, Crafts, and Wisdom

Muses: Goddesses of Inspiration

Nephthys: Goddess of the Tomb; also Goddess of Cleverness

Sarasvati: Goddess of Eloquence

Selene: Goddess of the Night and Moon

Syn: Goddess of Doors and Entrances

Thor: God of Lightning

Venus: Goddess of Love

Vesta: Goddess of Hearth, Home, and Fire

INDEX